AN
EASY-READ
FACT
BOOK

Trailbikes

David Jefferis

Franklin Watts

London   New York   Toronto   Sydney

©1984 Franklin Watts Ltd

First published in Great Britain
    1984 by
Franklin Watts Ltd
12a Golden Square
London W1

First published in the USA by
Franklin Watts Inc.
387 Park Avenue South
New York
N.Y. 10016

UK ISBN: 0 86313 079 8
US ISBN: 0-531-04709-1
Library of Congress Catalog Card
    Number: 83-50595

Photographs supplied by
All Sport
Dave Cannon
DPPI
Mark Moylan

Illustrated by
Hayward Art Group
Michael Roffe

Technical consultant
Dave Calderwood

The publishers wish to thank the
Stevenage Schoolboy
Scrambling Club and the Dear
family for their co-operation and
assistance.

Printed in Great Britain by
    Cambus Litho, East Kilbride

Trailbikes

Contents

The world of motorcycles

△ Off-road action! The start of an exciting motocross scramble. Racers like these have no unecessary items. To ride trailbikes on highways, lights, horn and indicators are needed.

There are many types of motorcycle, each used for a different purpose. They come in two main groups, those designed for riding on the highway and those designed for riding on bumpy off-road trails.

Sleek, big-engined superbikes are kings of the road and racing track. They often have plastic bodywork to smooth out the rushing blast of air at

high speeds. You can see a racing bike in the picture on the right.

Off-road trail machines look very different, as the bikes in the picture on the left show. They are not built for very high speeds, so have no wind-cheating bodywork. They have to keep going through thick mud and dust, so are equipped with thick knobby tires to give lots of grip.

△ This is a bike made for speeding around race tracks. The smooth bodywork protects the rider from the blast of the wind.

Off-road rider

Fuel tank will not spill if overturned

High-mounted mudguard

Race number

Engine

Shock absorber soaks up bumps and thumps

△ This is a typical off-road bike, designed for racing at motocross events. Head, tail and indicator lights are needed if the rider wants to go on the highway.

All off-road bikes share some common features.

Thick knobby tires with deep treads give grip in the mud.

High-mounted engines, sometimes with a "bash plate," allow a rider to go over rocks and bumps. Exhaust pipes are high-mounted for the same reason.

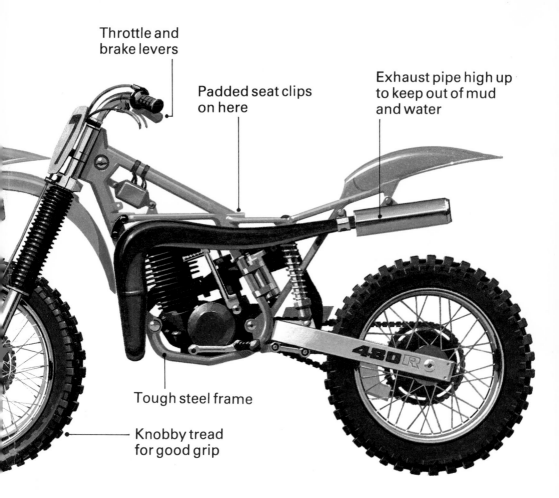

Throttle and
brake levers

Padded seat clips
on here

Exhaust pipe high up
to keep out of mud
and water

Tough steel frame

Knobby tread
for good grip

To soak up the bumps, shock absorbers have a long "travel." Mudguards are mounted high up too, and this prevents a buildup of mud between guard and tire.

Fuel tanks are usually of the non-spill type, so that gasoline does not overflow if the rider falls off the bike.

Powerhouse!

The heart of a motorcycle is its powerful engine.

Inside the engine is one or more pistons, each of which moves up and down inside a cylinder.

Fuel, a mixture of air and gasoline, is sucked into the top of the cylinder. Here, the high-voltage flash of an electric spark plug ignites the mixture, making it explode.

The explosion forces the piston down the cylinder. This is called the "power" stroke. As the piston moves down, it turns a crankshaft by a connecting rod which joins the piston and crankshaft together.

The turning motion of the crankshaft goes to the rear wheel through gears and a heavy metal chain.

Motorcycle engines can be of either two-stroke or four-stroke design. On these pages you can see how each type of engine works.

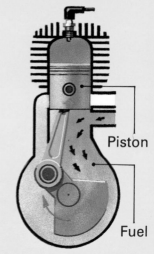

Two-stroke power

Piston

Fuel

Piston moves up cylinder.
Fuel sucked in below.

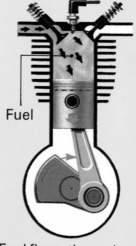

Four-stroke power

Fuel

Fuel flows through intake valve.

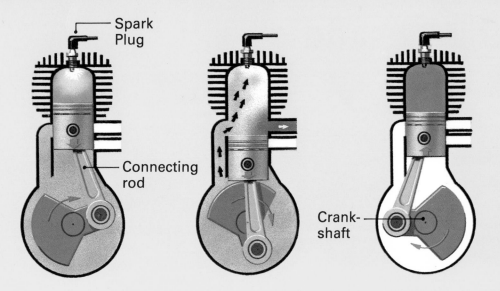

Power stroke. Piston moves down the cylinder.

Fuel flows in above piston. Burned gas flows out.

Piston starts to move up, ready for next power stroke.

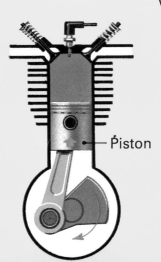

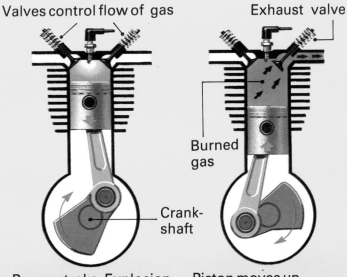

Piston moves up the cylinder.

Power stroke. Explosion pushes piston down.

Piston moves up, pushing burned gas out.

9

In the saddle

△ Here you see the handlebar layout of a motorcycle. The clutch lever is on the rider's left; throttle and front brake lever on the right. Motorcycles suitable for road-riding have speedometer and other instruments in the middle.

At first glance a motorbike looks a very complicated piece of machinery. But almost all motorcycles share the same control layout, which is quite easy to learn.

On the right handlebar is the twist-grip throttle. This controls the engine power – twist it toward you for more power, away for less. A finger's length away is the brake lever. Pulling this applies the front brake.

On the left handlebar there is another lever, the clutch. This is pulled in every time you change gears.

Under your left foot is the gearshift. Low gears are for starting and low speeds; high gears are for cruising.

Under your right foot is another brake lever. Pushing this applies the rear-wheel brake. The positions of other controls, such as lights and horn, vary from bike to bike.

△ These two pictures show the positions of the gearshift pedal (left) and the rear brake pedal (right).

Knobbies and shocks

▽ Many road bikes now have alloy wheels. Trailbikes still use spokes because they absorb the shocks of a rough ride better.

All trailbikes have thick, "knobby" tires and powerful shock absorbers.

Tires with very deep tread patterns are essential if you want to be able to ride along off-road trails. The tires of a road bike have shallower treads, de-

signed to give maximum grip on a smooth highway surface. Once in thick mud, a road bike's tires spin uselessly.

Good shock absorbers are vital for off-road action. Most bikes have four, a pair for each wheel. The latest bikes have a single rear shock absorber, which saves weight. Without shock absorbers, both bike and rider would be shaken to pieces.

▷ This cutaway picture shows the main parts of a shock absorber. **1** Oil in steel cylinder. **2** Piston moves up and down with spring. Oil slows it down, absorbing the bounciness of the spring. **3** Thick steel spring takes the shocks of the bumpy trail.

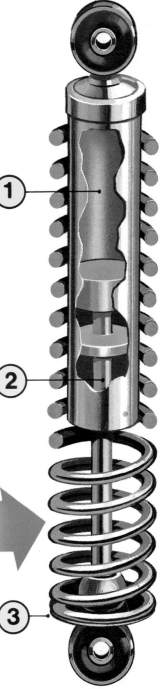

▽ This picture shows the rear shock absorber position. Front shocks are inside the forks, joining handlebars to front wheel.

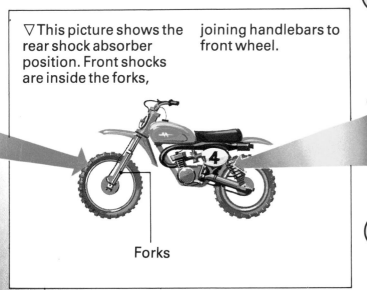

Forks

13

Leather and plastic

Trail riding is fun, but it can be dangerous too. Any fall can cause an injury, so good protection is vital.

The head is the most vulnerable part of your body, so a top-class helmet should always be worn. For high strength, modern helmets use several layers of fiberglass, plastic or nylon. Inside the outer shell is a thick layer of shock-absorbing polystyrene plastic and sometimes cork. The innermost lining is comfortably padded.

Your helmet must fit properly, as a loose one could fall off in an accident. The best way to get a helmet of the right size is to go along to your local motorcycle dealer who will see you are properly fitted out.

Leather is still the best protection for your arms and legs, though shoulder, elbow and knee protectors are usually of hard plastic. Boots have metal end-caps to stop them wearing out.

▷Here you see a rider, race-ready for a moto-cross event. For ordinary trail-riding you do not need to be quite so well dressed!

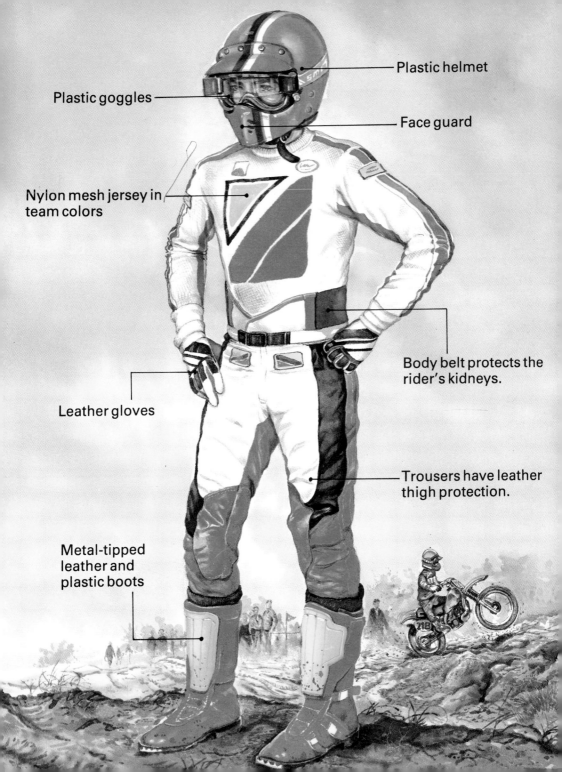

Plastic helmet

Plastic goggles

Face guard

Nylon mesh jersey in
team colors

Leather gloves

Body belt protects the
rider's kidneys.

Trousers have leather
thigh protection.

Metal-tipped
leather and
plastic boots

Early bikes

△ **1** The steam-powered bike by Michaux in 1869. **2** The world's first commercially made bike, the Hildebrand and Wolfmuller of 1894.

Today's reliable machines are a far cry from the efforts of the first motorcycle designers.

Ernest Michaux, a Frenchman, built a steam-powered bike in 1869. It was very slow, and gave riders a bumpy time, as it had solid tires. The first motorcycle made commercially was the Hildebrand and Wolfmuller of

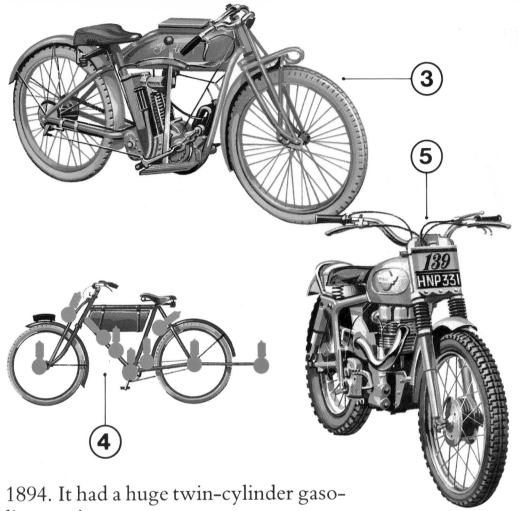

1894. It had a huge twin-cylinder gasoline engine.

Early machines had engines in various places – designers had different
ideas as to the best position. The Wer-
ner of 1901 was the first production
bike with an engine between the
wheels. Other makers followed, and
today all motorcycles have this layout.

△3 A classic early
American bike, the
Indian of 1901.
4 Early bikes had
engines in various
places, some of which
are shown by the red
outlines.
5 By the 1950s bikes like
this British Matchless
were world-beaters.

17

Trials riding

△▷ This picture, and the one opposite, show the sort of ground trials riders have to cover. All without putting a foot on the ground!

Trials riders have to battle their way across the roughest kind of country. Trials organizers plan routes along rocky stream beds, over steep hillsides and through deep muddy hollows. Riders try to complete these courses without stopping or putting a foot down to the ground.

Each course has a number of sections, with observers standing by to check the riders' progress. If a rider loses his balance and has to put a foot down, the observer marks points against him. If the rider stops, falls off or goes off-course, more points are marked down. At the end of the event, the rider with the fewest penalty points wins.

Unlike other motorcycle sports, speed is not the essential – what makes a winner is skill and a fine sense of balance.

Motocross

△ The first bend of a race is packed with riders, all jostling for a place. The last ones through have to ride in the dust and muck thrown up by the leaders.

Motocross is probably the most exciting motorcycle sport you can watch. Riders hammer their way around twisty circuits, flying through the air as they hit bumps. For protection, they wear plastic body armor, like modern-day jousting knights. Dust and dirt is spewed out from under spinning tires, often all over the onlooking spectators a few feet from the rutted track.

△ Hakan Carlqvist of
Sweden, racing at the
1983 British Grand Prix.
His speed won him the
race against riders from
15 countries.

▷ This Japanese Suzuki
is a typical motocross
bike. Like other
manufacturers, Suzuki
makes a range of off-
road bikes to suit
anyone, from beginners
to race-winners.

Enduros

△ This map shows the route of the Baja 1000. The pit stops are used for rest and repairs. Between pits, riders have to do repairs themselves. The 1982 two-man team rode a Honda XR500 to victory. They rode the 983.52 miles (1,583 km) in 17 hours 25 minutes.

An enduro is a long-distance race against time and rough country. Riders set off at one-minute intervals and race against the clock to average a set speed and arrive at a checkpoint on time.

Two of the toughest enduros are the Baja 1000 and the Paris–Dakar rally.

The Baja 1000 course snakes down through the burning heat and desert wastes of the Baja peninsula, Mexico. Throwing up long plumes of dust behind them, riders battle the heat, flat tires, crumbly roads and deep sand.

The Paris–Dakar rally is the biggest and longest enduro in the world. By the time riders have ridden through France, across much of the Sahara desert, and finally to Dakar on the west African coast, they have covered over 6,371 miles (10,250 km) in 20 days of racing and special tests. Not surprisingly there are accidents. In 1982 one rider crashed 10 times in one day . . . .

▷ A BMW four-stroke bike roars across the African desert on the Paris-Dakar rally. This bike went on to win the race. Strict rules ensure competitors keep the advertising slogans clean!

▽ Tire repairs under the burning African sun.

Other off-road events

△ Here you see a speedway race. Riders lean right over in the bends, spinning the rear tires in the dirt. Each race is just four laps long.

There are lots of other off-road motorcycle sports. Speedway racing is one of the most popular. In a race, four riders ride round a 400 meter (437 yard) track. Their bikes have just one gear and no brakes!

The track is loose cinders over a solid base and is carefully prepared for racing. Riders broadside their bikes round corners, boots scraping in the dirt, as

they struggle to keep their balance.

In east Europe and Scandinavia, ice racing is a popular motorcycle sport. The track is solid ice. For grip, tires are studded with wicked-looking 1¼ in (3 cm) steel spikes. Riders pad their knees and elbows with lengths of old tire as protection, both against spikes and the ice, as they lean the bikes nearly flat on the corners.

△ Ice racers roar around an almost circular course. Riders lean on sections of tire strapped to the left knee as they go around.

Riding your bike

△ A course like this includes similar features to a proper motocross course. Hills, bumps, gullies and sharp bends are all included. Practice on a small course like this will help you get going on long trail rides or in junior motocross events.

Riding a trailbike is a good way to start motorcycling. You can learn to handle the bike without any danger from cars and trucks. You can start earlier too – most countries will not allow riders on the road until they are teenagers.

Most towns have a local motorcycle club. Your dealer should have its address. Clubs are worth joining, as they give lots of friendly help and advice. Many hold regular junior motocross races too.

△ The first thing to learn is the layout of the various controls on the bike.

△ Smooth hill starts require a careful balance of throttle, clutch and brake.

△ Even though you are off-road, start practicing signals, ready for road-riding later on.

△ Riding fast is easy on a bike, riding slowly is much more difficult. Practice around obstacles like this.

Your first bike

Don't choose a bike which is too big or heavy for you. You will find it hard to control properly. Seat height is important – you must be able to touch the ground with the tips of both feet when you are seated.

Most of the trailbikes shown on these pages are "street-legal." This means that they have lights, indicators and a horn. To ride off-road, you need none of these.

Whichever bike you choose, learn to ride it properly and take care!

△ These junior moto-cross bikes are ideal for beginners under 10 years old.

Kawasaki AE50
Super motocross looks. The similar styled KE100 is available in the US.

Suzuki TS125
Good bike from Suzuki's wide range of off-road machines.

Yamaha DT125LC
Water-cooled machine, with good road performance.

Honda XL125S
Has a lower seat than many 125 bikes with room enough for two people.

Puch Ranger TT
Nicely styled bike from a European maker.

Glossary

Here is a list of some of the technical words in this book

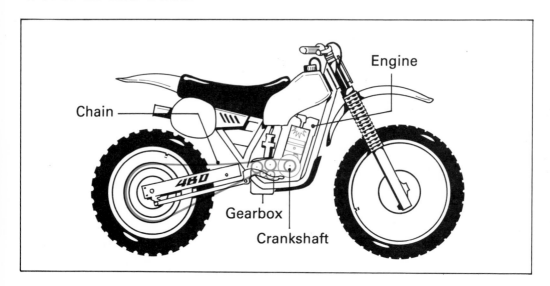

Engine

Chain

Gearbox

Crankshaft

△ The drawing above shows how a motorcycle works. Whatever their looks, all bikes work in a similar way.

The movement of the piston turns the crankshaft. A thick chain joins this to the gearbox. From the gearbox, another chain loops to join the back wheel, so turning it round.

Clutch
Allows power to be fed gradually from engine to gearbox, or to be disconnected for gear changing. The clutch is operated by pulling on a lever on the left handlebar.

Crankshaft
Rotating shaft joined to piston by a connecting rod. It changes the "up and down" movement of the piston to a circular motion that powers the motorcycle.

Cylinder
Part of the engine in which the piston moves. Bikes have various numbers of cylinders, depending on the design.

30

Drive chain
Thick metal chain, joins gearbox to rear wheel.

Rider's dictionary

Here are some words you will get to know in the world of motorcycles.

Four stroke
Type of engine which uses four strokes of the piston for each "power" stroke. Valves are used to let gas in and out of the cylinder.

Gearbox
Used to take power from crankshaft to drive chain. Bikes have four, five or six gears. Low gears are for starting or steep hills. High gears are for faster speeds.

Shock absorber
Device to smooth the bumps of off-road travel.

Spark plug
Electric device which screws into top of cylinder. When electricity is passed through it, it gives off a powerful spark, which makes gas in the cylinder explode.

Two stroke
Type of engine which does not use valves to move gas inside the engine. Has a "power" stroke every second stroke of the piston.

Blue groove track
Found in very hot, dry conditions. Rubber from tires lays down a blue slippery line around the track.

Broadside
Cornering like a speedway rider, back end out and tire spinning. Riders balance bike with their foot, sliding it on the track.

Floater
Type of rear suspension using a single gas-filled shock absorber.

Designated trail
Off-road trail, on which trailbikers can legally ride their machines. Many trails are only for walkers or horses.

Forks
Long pair of tubes which join the front wheel to

the rest of the bike. Inside are shock absorbers.

Lid
Helmet

Moto-X
Or MX; short for Moto-Cross

Pit
Special area, used in races, where mechanics can work on a bike. Repairs can be carried out and fuel loaded.

"Road rash"
Scraped skin caused by a fall on paved surface.

Wheelie
Lifting a bike off its front wheel, still keeping control. Dave Taylor, a stunt rider, once rode an arm-wrenching 38 miles (61 km) "pulling a wheelie" all the way.

31

Index